To Serve is Love

Annie Jiggetts

Copyright © 2016 by Annie Jiggetts

To Serve is Love
by Annie Jiggetts

Printed in the United States of America.

ISBN 9781498481533

All rights reserved solely by the author. The author guarantees all contents are original and do not infringe upon the legal rights of any other person or work. No part of this book may be reproduced in any form without the permission of the author. The views expressed in this book are not necessarily those of the publisher.

Scripture quotations taken from the King James Version (KJV) – *public domain*

www.xulonpress.com

Table of Contents

Phase 1 9
Phase 2 13
Phase 3 17
Phase 4 19
Phase 5 21

Welcome to my life: the good and bad, paths not taken in life, unfulfilled dreams, goals, achievements, lack of encouragement and support from those who claimed they cared and loved me. However, I'm grateful I found out God has all the love I'll ever need, at times when I felt I didn't fit in with my family or peers. I am sixty-one years old and have been in ministry since the age of eight. Sit with me as I share some of the spiritual awakenings that made me want to spend my life being a servant. God inspired me to share my testament in hopes that it will encourage you to seek Jesus Christ for yourself—find He who saves, delivers, heals, and sets free. This could not be possible without the abiding of the Holy Spirit, so I claim no credit for the lessons taught as I live life. My purpose is as a humble servant of God, and my desire is to encourage others to live for Him and Him alone.

As a eulogy to my past, what's dead should stay buried. My hope is that my journey will help others stop living in their past also. Sin blocks the flow of God's blessings in life; the Bible says in Romans 3:23, "For all have sinned and come short of the glory of God." I ask as you're reading these pages that it will encourage you to live for Christ.

Why don't you get a drink and let's get acquainted, shall we? Let's start with a prayer from the Word in Ephesians 3:16-21 (KJV):

> Heavenly Father; I come to you now in the Name of our Lord and Savior Jesus Christ. I ask You to strengthen our inner man with might through Jesus Christ, that through faith, Christ may dwell in our hearts; that we are rooted and grounded in love, and

we may be able to comprehend with all the saints what is the width and length and depth and height; and to know the love of Christ, which passeth knowledge; that we may be filled with all the fullness of You, Heavenly Father. I thank you that Jesus Christ is able to do exceedingly abundantly above all that we ask or think according to the power that works in us, unto Him be glory in the church by Jesus Christ to all generations, forever and ever. Amen!

Phase 1

I was born and named Annie Louse Jiggetts in the early morning of God's tender mercies by a midwife in a rural country town in the USA. Not a by-product of wedded bliss, I had a mother I wasn't told about until the age of twelve and an absent father, who to date still hasn't been active in my life. I was never legally adopted, but my mother gave me away to a family member and his wife when I was still a toddler. My rearing began in a second floor apartment above the church I grew up in. Being raised by these relatives was the beginning of some of the worst years I'd endure: molesting, fondling, beatings, incest and rapes started when I was barely five, and continued repeatedly until I was nineteen by relatives, so-called "family friends," co-workers, and acquaintances.

The first time happened with my step-mom's brother, who was staying at our house and at times was my babysitter. He drank and would sit me on his lap and fondle me. Of course, being a child at the time, I had no clue what he was doing to me. At times, he poured a little beer in my bottle, so I would go right to sleep after he was done. This went on for a while, and then it escalated as I got older.

One night, he came in late drunk and snuck into my bedroom, which was right next to my parents' room. That was the first time he penetrated me. The pain was unbearable. I remember trying to scream so my parents would wake up, but as soon as I did, he put his hand over my mouth, so nobody came to my rescue. Afterward, I saw blood and when I tried to get up, I could barely move my legs because it felt like something was torn inside me. I was only twelve and my virginity was gone before I was old enough to learn what that meant. Yet, that didn't seem to matter to him because he kept finding ways to violate me over and over again.

These episodes caused a flood of emotions: anger, confusion, depression, uselessness, and worthlessness. This takes me to 2 Corinthians 10:3-5 that says:

> For though we walk in the flesh, we do not war after the flesh; for the weapons of our warfare are not carnal, but mighty through God to the pulling down of strong holds. Casting down imaginations, and every high thing that exalteth itself against the knowledge of God, and bringing into captivity every thought to the obedience of Christ.

Strange as it may sound, I've always felt a strong presence overshadowing me, which later in life I would learn was the Holy Spirit of Jesus Christ. I accepted Him into my heart and was baptized when I was eight years old. However, for many years during the abuse, the enemy, who the Word taught me was Satan, deceived me into believing I was of no worth and deserved all the unspeakable things being done to me. John 10:10(a) says it best: "The thief [Satan] cometh not, but for to steal, and to kill, and to destroy." Once I allowed my mind to be deceived by Satan and slip into depression, the doorway was opened and he held me in captivity.

After the abuse had escalated to rape, I sank deep into darkness to the point that I was numb to life and stopped caring one way or the other. I may have accepted Christ early in life, but I was too hurt and lost to seek out a relationship with Him. While in one of my darkest hours, I began to think of revengeful ways to get back at the people who took what should have been some of the best years of my life. As a result, I became rebellious and angry most of the time. All I wanted was a way out of the torment. When I was twelve, I thought of ways to hurt them as they had hurt me. I was so depressed that the thoughts of suicide and murder were sounding pretty good.

Yet, every time the opportunity presented itself, there was that overpowering presence of the Holy Spirit again, reminding me what John 15:4(a) says: "Abide in me, and I in you."

Hebrews 13:5(b)-6 says, "For He hath said, 'I will never leave thee, nor forsake thee.' So that we may boldly say, 'The Lord is my helper, and I will not fear what man shall do unto me.'" What I didn't realize then was the Lord was my protector through it all. He could rescue me from myself if I would just be still and focus on Him, instead of trying to do what I thought I could do on my own. Then, I would come out as the victor instead of the victim.

Why do we try to fight battles when God clearly states we don't have to? "For the battle is not yours, but God's" (2 Chronicles 20:15(b). Sorry to say I wasn't out of the valley yet because I still wasn't listening to God speaking to me in the midst of my storms.

During those years, I let Satan convince me I wasn't worthy of God's love, grace, or tender mercies. I had made up in my mind that since men repeatedly took my body for their pleasures physically, and not being strong enough to fight them off. I was always threatened never to tell anyone or else worse would happen the next time. I decided I should use it to my advantage and get compensated for the pieces of my life men stole over and over again, whether monetarily or through material goods. I was lost, foolish, and did not care what happened to myself. I allowed my body to be sold out for the Devil. This give-and-take continued up until my mid-twenties. I was jacked-up that long. Believe me when I say the sins of my flesh have truly cost me at a price I had no clue I'd have to pay. I'm still paying for some of the wrong choices I've made by allowing my body to be used and abused physically and mentally by men. Whoever said, "Confession is good for the soul," hit the nail on the head. At the time I really believed I hadn't committed any sins, but God said it best in 1 John 1:8-10:

> If we claim to be without sin, we deceive ourselves and the truth is not in us. If we confess our sins, He is faithful and just and will forgive us our sins and cleanse us from all unrighteousness. If we say that we

have not sinned, we make Him out to be a liar and His Word has no place in our lives.

He also said in John 8:32, "And ye shall know the truth, and the truth shall make you free." I've since learned that telling the truth will keep you free. What blessed assurance that is.

Phase 2

The first time I heard a word from the Lord, His voice was gentle and called me by name. It was on October 26, 1994 at 5:10 a.m. and I was forty years old. I was asleep at home and awakened by these words: "

"Get thee to a place where I can establish thee and I shall prepare thee for a work. Be no longer tossed, search no more. I have appointed thee for such a time as this. By my hands and my works shall ye be covered. 'Peace be unto thee'; said the Lord of Hosts. I have adorned thee. My hands are upon thee. I shall raise thee up and prosper thee. No longer shall thou eat from the dust of the earth. I shall make thee the head; and not the tail; and thou shalt be above only, and thou shalt not be beneath; if that thou hearken unto my commandments, which I command thee this day, to observe and to do them." Deut.28:13(KJV) 'Heaven smiles upon thee;' saith the Lord. See my works, thou art a blessed servant in whom I am pleased. Hold fast and glorious shall be thy works. Be of good cheer and the joy I give thee shall be thy strength. I shall give thee great joy. I shall send thee word of the place thou shalt go. I shall strengthen thee. Just do my will and ye shall be blessed abundantly. I shall strengthen thee. I shall strengthen thee; saith the Lord.

Then His voice stopped. My body trembled the whole time. I couldn't believe I was actually hearing God. It was beyond amazing.

I also remember the first vision I had. It was around midnight on October 14, 1995, at the age of forty-one. I was in my car, talking with a fellow believer, when my eyes were drawn to the sky above the house. The moon was full and bright, when all of a sudden, one mass of clouds moved swiftly. As it covered the moon, it began to take a different form. I felt a warmth come over me. Then, to my amazement, the clouds stopped, and in the middle I saw a soft beam of light, which at first I thought was the moon shining through them. Then I saw an outline that resembled the shape of a face. The eyes glowed and looked to the east with a smile. Just as quickly as I had seen the form, the clouds went back to the way they were before this and I could see the moon again, as if nothing had been disturbed. I felt as though God was pleased another lost soul had been saved somewhere in the world, right at that moment. Hallelujah! I don't know why I was allowed to see this, but I thanked Him in my heart and rejoiced with my mouth in praise. Isn't God awesome?

I had another vision on September 4, 1997. It was mid-morning and I was putting the kitchen back in order after getting my sons Josh and Joseph off to school. I turned on the TV and sat down in the living room to watch a rerun of *Little House on the Prairie*. It was the episode where Michael Landon read the story of Jesus's birth to his children on Christmas Eve. There was a severe snow blizzard in this particular episode, which had left a man dead. All of a sudden, I wasn't in the living room anymore. That overwhelming presence came over me again and I saw myself in a hospital emergency room looking at my first-born son lying on a gurney. He appeared to be wounded. His godmother was there to comfort me as I cried on her shoulder. As the tears filled my eyes, I felt something pass through me. I still to this day can't put it into words, but it was as real as my telling you this testament right now. I believed in my heart that God would show me what this vision meant in His own time, not mine. I prayed that day it wouldn't be my son, but nevertheless, "thy will be done."

    I am sad to say, that vision did become a reality in his senior year of high school while he was staying with his dad. He was wounded by gunfire at a park basketball game. When I received the call, though shook up, my mind reflected back to the vision I had prior to this incident. Even though I had shared with my son what I had seen and forewarned him to be more aware when he's out of the house, it wasn't enough to prevent it from happening. Thanks be to God for bringing him through, still alive and well. Every time I think of the goodness of Jesus, and all He's done and is still doing in my life, my heart starts to dance. He is the center of all my joy, the depth of all my days and the height of all my nights. Nothing can compare to what Jesus brings to the fibers of my soul. He rocks this vessel 24/7.

Phase 3

My thoughts often go back to some things I wrote to Jesus in one of my journals back on June 28, 2003, when I didn't feel His presence:

Hello Lord, I missed you today. I didn't feel that closeness I'd sensed with me all the time. I know you do an awful lot in the course of a 24 hour day, so if I'm sounding a bit selfish, forgive me. You know it's only because I love you so, don't you? Thanks for being the Almighty One you are to me and to the world around me. The more I think of how wonderful, forgiving, loving, and precious you are, the more I love and thank you for saving me, for you're always there. You never leave me; I leave you. I enjoy the intimate times we share because you always listen and advise me on any subject, even when it's silly or I am babbling on about something or a whole lot of nothing. You keep me alive day after day. I am forever indebted to you, Lord. Since He knows what I'm thinking before I say it, it wouldn't make any sense to try and hide anything from Him because He's higher than I. His Word tell us in Isaiah 55:8-9, "For my thoughts are not your thoughts, neither are your ways my ways;' saith the Lord. 'For as the heavens are higher than the earth, so are my ways higher than your ways and my thoughts than your thoughts.'" I'm so glad about it, saints, and you should be too! I believe if we spent more time loving instead of judging others, because we all have fallen short, then we can truly be called children of God. He instructs us not to judge in Matthew 7:1-2: "Judge not, that ye be not judged. For in the same way you judge others, you will be judged, and with the measure you use, it will be measured to you."

Well, I heard that same voice saying; "I didn't promise you that dark clouds would not hover over your life, or that the future would bring you many rainbows. Nor that every tomorrow would be perfect, or life on earth would be easy, because trials and tribulations would come. I did promise to see you through and I'd never leave you alone. I promised I would always be there for you, to listen and to help you through any circumstance. I also promised to give you in this life now and forever my undying love, hope, strength and encouragement you need to carry on. I also promised to supply all of your needs. Just ask me."

After hearing this, I thought, *that's what real love is*. Jesus picked me up and turned me around at my lowest point in life. You know, if God can love me in spite of my faults, then I should be willing to make every effort to follow His pattern for my life, wouldn't you say? I was able to sleep well after that. I hope this is soul-stirring for you.

I can recall getting some of what I called "proverbial wisdom" back then such as, "the worth of a real man shows in the countenance of his of his mate's face." True vision comes from the heart. Courage, friendship, faith, and love may not be seen, but it's everything. As a white candle in a holy place, so is the beauty of an aged face. This applies to those who have served the Lord all their earthly lives, and are still bearing the fruits of their labor in their latter years. Wrinkles stand for earnest times of prayer, loving care, and decades of useful work. Beauty is no longer the skin-deep charm of youth, but the time-honored loveliness of a life well lived in constant service unto God.

Let's wrap up on a different note about some advice that was told to me by various wise folks along this journey called life. One described it this way: "Work like you don't need the money, love like you've never been hurt, dance like no one is watching, and live as if this day is your last." To be truly happy in a relationship, two people should seek to compliment, not complete each other. They should appreciate and celebrate their differences as well as things they have in common.

Phase 4

Do you ever think about life as being a reflection of the state you're in at the time? You'd be amazed at what you can see. I've had these thoughts a few times, and the one particular reply that I received back in 2003 was, "My life is rich and full in meaningful and deeply satisfying ways all because of God's agape love for me." On an obvious note, most of us desire the sparks of love and passion that are found with that special someone who takes your breath away; someone who gives you the heart-pounding feeling of mutual bonding two people share when they're together and the comforting measure of abiding respect and true love that's acknowledged by the two.

I remember the first man I thought I was in love with and married back in the fall of 1978. I'd known him since childhood; we grew up in the same neighborhood and our families knew each other, but I had never looked at him in that way until he came home from the war in those dress blues. I was in the military at the time also. At first, I thought I married him for love after he had proposed numerous times. Then I came to see him as an escape from the abusive life I was in. So I finally said yes to get away from it all, which was a huge mistake. Instead of leaning on Jesus to rescue me, I thought I had the power to fix it myself. What a wrong choice I made. The first few years were, as the world calls it, "wedded bliss," and after that I felt like I had stepped in quicksand and was sinking quickly. That's what happens when we think we know what's best for us more than God does and we don't wait on Him. It resulted in our union taking a turn for the worst. Returning home from the war ended up having negative effects on our marriage mentally and physically, and I had no clue as to how to help us or deal with any of it. However, I'm grateful to say God delivered me out of darkness into His marvelous light.

The best that came from that partnership were two wonderful sons who are the jewels in my crown. Their births brought so much joy to my life and taught me how to truly love after the marriage ended in 1988. I'm so thankful to be saved by God's grace.

Phase 5

*S*ince maturing in my walk with God, I have the privilege of being a godmother and spiritual role model to a lot of other children and their families.

Now, let's get to the best subject, which is my favorite: Love. God showed me and taught me about His unwavering love in 1 Corinthians 13:4-8(a):

> Love is patient; love is kind. It doesn't envy, it doesn't boast, it's not proud. It's not rude; it's not self-seeking; it's not easily angered; it keeps no record of wrongs. Love doesn't delight in evil, but rejoices with the truth. Love always protects, always trusts, always hopes, always perseveres. Love never fails.

Now, let's get deep. Have we forgotten the true depth of God's love? Or perhaps we never knew it. Is it possible those who shaped and molded our lives in this world were so busy feeding, clothing, and protecting us that they missed the basics, the foundation, and the pattern of life—that there's nothing greater than love? All that comes from God will return to Him. Have we been blinded by the masks and postures that make us feel loved and loveable, or the temptations and lusts that make us feel good when we don't? What about the excitement and enjoyment that help us forget the pieces of ourselves that we've given away for a few moments of passion and pleasure, or life's struggles and the pain we feel when we mistake something else for love? How did we lose sight of the fact that love is all, nothing less than the fullness of God and His Word alone? Or have we disowned love because it once appeared to be a dark evasive shadow, showing us things that we didn't want to see about ourselves? Have we let the world deceive us about wanting to be loved and loving that it has left us loveless, lovelorn and craving love? Or maybe the simple explanation is that we've taken so much of God out of love, that we can no longer find ourselves in it? Consider this a lesson in life's reality.

Take this word of warning with you from Isaiah 5:20: "Woe unto those who call evil good and good evil."

I remember taking His grace and mercy for granted before He taught me how to see the truth. I've often wondered what life would be without His divine healing, words of wisdom, and the caring and loving way He touches and protects my heart, lifting me when I need it the most. Without Him, what would I be? Nonexistent. What would I gain? No eternal life in glory with Him. I couldn't fathom existing in a world where someone doesn't love me the way He does. He's the only one who ever understood and accepted me as I am. I know without a doubt that my Heavenly Father, is nothing short of omniscient. His infinite love. has and always will be life's greatest gift to me.

Lord, you are the first one I think of each morning when I rise and the last one I think of each night when I close my eyes. You let me rest in your bosom, where I feel most protected. Oh, how I love you, Jesus. All you've imparted in me through the years keeps me humble before thee.

As we grow up, we learn the people who weren't supposed to ever let us down probably will. We will have our hearts broken, likely more than once, and getting past it doesn't get any easier. We may fight with our best friends and neighbors, or blame a new love for things an ex-love did. We may cry because time is passing too fast and we'll eventually lose a loved one. So take too many photos, laugh a lot, and love like you've never been hurt. Because every second you spend upset is a second of happiness you'll never get back. So don't be afraid life will end; be afraid it will never begin.

Listen, the time is now if you believe the Word of God. Love Him now while you can. Know the sweet and tender mercies from

Phase 5

which true love flows. Love Him now while He's here with you. It will be too late when you're gone from this world and then have sweet words chiseled on an ice-cold marble headstone. If you have tender thoughts of Him, please tell Him now. If you wait until you're sleeping, never to awaken, there will be death between you and you won't hear Him then. So if you say you love Jesus, even a little bit, let Him know it while the blood is still running warm in your veins, so He can hear it.

God created the fountains to mingle with the rivers and the rivers with the oceans. The winds of heaven mix forever with sweet motions. Nothing in the world is single.

I recall the times I didn't feel His presence with me, or so I thought, before He told me in Deuteronomy 31:6(b), "He will never leave you nor forsake you."

I also learned that life isn't peaches and crème. Even in my pit of sins, which was the worst times in my life, because I was always so full of anger, resentment, and rebellion for all the years of abuse I endured with the help of my Savior. Yet, through it all I learned to totally depend on God and His Word. By doing so, I've gained wisdom, knowledge, understanding, and love—that's priceless.

He's also taught me how to love others unconditionally in spite of themselves because people come into our lives for a reason, a season, or a lifetime. When we've figured out which one it is, we know exactly how to live. Those who come into our lives for a reason are usually there to meet a need we have expressed outwardly or inwardly. They come to assist us through difficulties, to provide guidance, support and to aid us physically, emotionally and spiritually. They appear to be a Godsend, which some are, and they are there for the reasons you need them to be. Then, without any wrongdoing on your part, or at an inconvenient time, this person will say or do something to bring the relationship to an end. Some walk away, some act up or out, and force you to take a stand. What we must realize is our needs are met and our desires are fulfilled. Their work is done and the prayers we sent up have been answered, so it is now time to move on. The people that come into our lives for a season, because our turn has come to share, grow, and learn, may bring us an experience of peace or make us laugh. They may teach us something we've never tried. They usually give us an unbelievable amount of joy. Believe it! It's real, but only for a season.

Lifetime relationships teach us long-lasting lessons—those things we must build upon in order to have a solid foundation. Our job is to accept the lessons, love the person anyway, and put what we've learned to use in all the other relationships and areas of our lives. Yesterday is history. Tomorrow is a mystery. Every day is a gift from the Creator. That's why it's called the circle of life. So love people and use things—do not use people and love things.

If this world were as concerned for their souls as they are about being someone other than the original, how truly wonderful our lives would be. I can never fathom why people find it acceptable to risk death to be acknowledged by this world, rather than strive to gain eternal life with God by living in obedience to His Word.

Let's step into another side regarding life that I learned about my dreams of marriage. Before you get married, keep both eyes open and after you say, "I do," close one eye. Before you get involved and make a commitment to anyone, don't let low self-esteem, pressure from others, ignorance, desperation, lust, or immaturity blind you to the warning signs. Don't let the Devil fool you into thinking you have the power to change someone, or that what you see as others' faults aren't that important. Once you make a decision to commit to someone, over time their differences, pet peeves, flaws, and vulnerabilities will become obvious. However, if you truly love your mate and want the relationship to grow and develop by natural process, you need to learn to close one eye and not take every tit for tat literally. You and your mate will have many different strengths, weaknesses, dreams, values, expectations, and emotional needs. You are two individuals uniquely created by God, who decided to share a journey together. Neither of you are perfect, but could be perfect for each other. Ask yourselves: do you control, compete, and compare? Do you compliment and compromise with each other? Do you bring out the best of each other? What do you bring to this union? Do you bring past hurt, pain, mistrust, and failed relationships? Do you keep exhuming the past to relive it in the present? You can't take someone to the altar to alter them, nor can you make anyone love you or stay with you. If you develop self-esteem, spiritual discernment, and "a life with Christ," you won't find yourself making others responsible for your happiness, pain, jealousy, control, manipulation, neediness, and selfishness. These aren't the characteristics for a thriving, loving, healthy, and lasting relationship. Seeking sex, wealth, status and security are the wrong reasons to be in a relationship. What keeps a relationship strong is trust, communication, intimacy, a sense of humor, sharing, some alone time, and daily exchanges (a shared activity, hug, meal, call, note, touch). Send a nice email or leave a message on their voicemail; share common goals and interests, because growth is progress in itself. To grow is what's important. So grow together, not apart, giving each other the space needed to grow without feeling insecure. Allow your mate to have outside interests. You can't be together every minute, unless you're in a fairytale. So give each other assurance of commitment and a sense of belonging. Don't waste precious moments trying to control one another when God is the one in control. Learn each other's family situation and respect each other's parents regardless. Don't pressure each other for material things. Remember "for richer or poorer," or as I say, "for God or Satan." If these qualities are missing, the relationship will erode eventually, as resentment, abuse, withdrawal, dishonesty, neglect, and pain replace the love. So always try to be a little more kindhearted than necessary. The difference between "untied" and "united" is where you put the "I."

    Well, as much as I love spending time wrapped up in you, Lord, let me close with one of my many favorite prayers for all of us who truly believe you are the Savior of the whole world. Before I pray, let's be real about who, what, and why we exist. The reality of the matter is God's churches come in all shapes and styles. They meet in homes, worship services, open gatherings in stadiums, and amphitheaters. They pack thousands into a sanctuary, while an overflowing crowd watches on closed circuit television worldwide. Buildings vary, but the church is made up of the saints of God, not the structures we gather in, and includes every race and nation who loves our Lord and have committed to serving Him. That being said, my prayer for you is one that Apostle Paul prayed for the Church of Ephesus, to strengthen the believers in their Christian faith by teaching them the nature (what) and purpose (why) of the body of Christ for you the church.

Let us pray together:

For this reason, I kneel before you Father, from whom His whole family in heaven and on earth derives its name. I pray that out of His glorious riches He may strengthen you with power through His Spirit in your inner being so that Christ may dwell in your hearts through faith. And I pray that you, being rooted and established in love, may have power, together with all the saints, to grasp how wide and long and high and deep is the love of Christ, and to know this love that surpasses knowledge—that you may be filled to the measure of all the fullness of God. Now to Him who is able to immeasurably more than we ask or imagine, according to His power that is at work within us, to Him be glory in the church and in Christ Jesus throughout all generations forever and ever. Amen. (Ephesians 3:14-21)

Thanks isn't nearly enough for all the continuous prayers, uplifting love and unwavering support through it all, without which I wouldn't have come this far in my walk. I love you, my God-given family, for what you mean to me. I'll close with a poem written about me in August 2015 by my neighbor and sister in Christ, Karen Doll, with her permission of course:

God's Soul Seeker

No matter the time of day, or the day of the week, there's a special person anyone can call upon. If you have a problem or need a good laugh or preaching on Sunday, I know the right person who will listen, help, and give lots of kisses and hugs. She's one of God's very own and she's always within reach. She's well known for passing out a tremendous amount of love and she loves to teach and preach. Her message is about life, Satan, and most of all, our loving God above. I hope you're never afraid to hear the truth, for that is what she speaks. It's when she receives the message from God, she has to move on. While in one place, her job is to seek lost souls, then out for them she'll reach, to share the Word, touch each person's soul, and to place a smile upon a frown. She's a very special person that rids of Satan as he cleverly creeps, with God in your soul, you will feel refreshed and full of love, then share it with others, since the Word of God has come within your reach to read each day. That's when the special part of your life God will play. I thank God for His blessed daughter and for all her love and teachings. I'd like to thank the one that blesses me throughout each day. I'm very proud to introduce to you God's loving daughter Mama J.

This testament was God-inspired and written by one of His works still in progress. *Hallelujah!*

www.ingramcontent.com/pod-product-compliance
Ingram Content Group UK Ltd.
Pitfield, Milton Keynes, MK11 3LW, UK
UKHW041957230426
12048UKWH00008B/387